# I DID IT ON PURPOSE

A 12 Day Devotional Workbook

IDiditOnPurpose.com

Copyright 2019 by Robyn-Ann Young. All rights reserved.
Published by UNCAGED Media.
ISBN: 978-0-9983405-6-2

12 days of Inspiration and journal prompts to help you refine your purpose and pursue it with passion.

**12**

**Devotionals**
**Quotes**
**Questions**
**Challenges**

**IDidItOnPurpose.com**

# INTRO

Hi Lionheart.

Welcome to the Purpose Challenge! Over the next 12 days you will finally be able to kick confusion to the curb and live each day like you mean it. Because if you're not doing things on purpose, you're doing them by accident - and ain't nobody got time for that!

Again, I'm Robyn-Ann, your fierce faith cheerleader reminding you that Jesus did not save you on layaway. **You were bought with a price for a purpose.**

I created this extended challenge for those serious about walking in godly confidence everyday. No matter your season or situation, God has spoken clearly on how to conduct yourself based on your kingdom identity and mission.

I've been there, where I felt so close to God in Sunday church yet so disconnected at Monday's work. Since then, I've learned to let God's words transform my circumstance, instead of letting my circumstance cloud God's words to me.

Jesus didn't save you to tame you, and Christianity is not a safe cage to box you into boredom. The culture is yours to impact. So let's take up the Word and **do it on purpose.**

*p.s. Instagram or Facebook me with the #IDidItOnPurposeChallenge tag so I know how you're doing. Or feel free to email me with any questions: hi@robyn-ann.com* ☺

## DAY 1

"Therefore do not be foolish, but understand what the will of the Lord is."

–Ephesians 5:17

Before going further, you must decide once and for all which team you're going to play for. That is the only way to establish which coach to listen to, and to know where you are going to end up.

So many times, we're lusting too much after the world to even notice God's moves on the field. Then when not on the bench, we wander into the game with lack of purpose and find ourselves asking "How far can I compromise without sinning?" rather than "How far can I go with God?"

If you still find yourself asking the former question frequently, you are most likely scoring points for the wrong team. Asking "How far is too far before its sin" will only produce a life where you keep getting pushed into the sin end zone. If godly sorrow is flooding your heart because you realize how much this wastes God's goodness, just pray and ask right now for His help to refocus.

## Jesus didn't save you on layaway.
Your purpose and success has already been fully paid for.

# CHALLENGE:

Ask God to remind you of the high price that was paid for your freedom and to turn your focus back to Him. Recommit to playing for His team and His purpose if you're going to wear the jersey of being "Christian".

# JESUS DIDN'T SAVE YOU ON LAYAWAY,
you were bought with a price for a purpose.

## Pinpoint Purpose:

What issues do you notice in the Christian culture that make you sad? Write down 2-3 things that concern you or sometimes push you away from churches. How can you act to improve one of these areas since you also represent the church to your peers?

_____

_____

_____

_____

_____

_____

_____

_____

_____

_____

## DAY 2

"Look carefully then how you walk, not as unwise but as wise, making the best use of the time, because the days are evil."

Now that you've repented for aimlessly wandering around on the field at tImes, let's get an understanding for the privileged position you've been called to on God's team. Like your Father, you operate from wisdom - knowing what to do in each situation. So you must refuse to sit down in lap of confusion.

However, true wisdom comes from knowing Jesus' words for yourself. Waiting 'til Sunday to hear the pastor preach will leave you clueless on what to do Monday through Saturday when you're alone.

Your time also becomes more valuable because you realize it's only been given to you for a specific reason. Another year will quickly pass, but instead of just waiting for Beyoncé or Drake to drop their next album, you will better know the Lord and understand your purpose – aka your goal and touchdown.

There is now a joy in knowing where you're headed and how to play to win.

**You know what you're saved for, so you don't wander back to what you were saved from.**

# CHALLENGE:

Spend some time in prayer meditating on why God has you at the job, church, or house where He's currently placed you. It will bring much more focus and productivity to your tasks.*

# KNOW WHAT YOU'RE SAVED FOR

or you'll only return to what you were saved from.

## Pinpoint Purpose:

What do you see or imagine when you pray and daydream? Write down a few of the recurring visions of yourself or society you notice when you let your mind wander.

_____

_____

_____

_____

_____

_____

_____

_____

## DAY 3

**Turn my eyes away from worthless things; preserve my life according to your word.**

*— Psalm 119:37*

# Your purpose doesn't care how you feel and neither should you.

It's time to stop babying your flesh. It is okay to tell your emotions "NO" at times to establish who's in control. As Romans 8:14 reminds us, your spirit man leads.

Yes, you have to live in the real world, but if there are any distractions that can be cut, it's time for them to go! And don't be apologetic about it either. Sometimes we're more concerned about missing out on earthly things than missing out on heaven-on-earth.
Even if something is not direct sin, it's often good to fast physical pleasures to be more in tune with your spiritual taste buds. It's like saying no to your coworker's junk food so you can preserve your appetite for mama's three course meal at home.

"All things are lawful," but not all things are helpful. "All things are lawful," but not all things build up (1 Corinthians 10:23). Perspective is everything. Therefore, you must frequently review the benefits that come with pursuing purpose. That way, you can quickly identify worthless relationships and habits that sometimes sneak back in.
Remind yourself that you can't afford to keep settling for good at the expense of great. **Ain't nobody got time for that!**

# CHALLENGE:

Write down a list of your closest friends (3-5). Do any of them know your purpose, or share the same vision to complete God's call on their life? If not, pray and ask God to give you favor with a new community of women, and a mentor that will draw His best out of you.*

# YOUR PURPOSE DOESN'T CARE HOW YOU FEEL,

and neither should you.

## Pinpoint Purpose:

Is there a common struggle or need you frequently notice when chatting with your friends? Write down what you wish you could do to help them if you had the time or resources.

_____

_____

_____

_____

_____

_____

_____

_____

_____

## DAY 4

"Leave the dead to bury the dead. But as for you, go and proclaim the kingdom of God."

*– Luke 9:60*

Let's put Jesus' words in a more current light. "Leave your coworker to rack up every certification known to man because corporate America can lay you off at any moment. But as for you, focus on excelling in exactly what I've called you to."

Of course, acquiring certifications are not sinful and are actually good to develop yourself in your committed field. But if motivated by fear or the worried culture around you, it becomes disobedience and a distraction to why God has positioned you where you are. You know that **pursuing purpose will bring the paper, not the other way around.**

Unlike those working for themselves, you know you are under the main contract of "advancing heaven into earth". So doors that God opens for you in a job, neighborhood, or creative team are opportunities to bring His light and prosperous worldview to that sphere of influence. Your main job description is to re-present Christ and His heart to those around you. What a privilege!

May your heavenly agenda be the fuel and strength you need to carry out this week's tasks with joy and focus. **Remember why you started.**

# CHALLENGE:

What's one thing you can do today to move forward in your purpose? Remind yourself of what excited you in the beginning, and create a list of steps towards that end goal. Breaking down the vision will help you last for the marathon, and not just a few sprints.*

# REMEMBER WHY YOU STARTED.

Pursue purpose, not paper.

## Pinpoint Purpose:

What advice do people always ask you for? Why do you think they see you as knowledgeable in these areas? Write down one way you can package this information so it can more readily be shared with the next person that asks.

_____

_____

_____

_____

_____

_____

_____

_____

_____

## DAY 5

"'Man shall not live by bread alone, but by every word that comes from the mouth of God.'"

*– Matthew 4:4*

Instead of falling into hopelessness when you fall short of your purpose, see it as your spirit man signaling you to eat! If you can no longer see the point for pursuing your passions, take stock to see when you last feasted on the Word of God.

Those Instagram quotes can only take you so far. We should taste and see that the Lord is good, but then continue chewing on the Word until we are full! If not, you neglect your spiritual appetite and eventually turn to your shallow emotional cravings in an attempt to scratch the itch.

Yet, unlike those in the world who sample random palettes trying to find what they're searching for – we know what our body needs. Don't envy the walking dead because they seem content on the world's junk food. Their frequent sugar highs also end in frequent empty lows. I mean, just listen to their roller coaster love songs. Constantly indulging in the next quick fix only ends in spiritual malnutrition and starvation.

Return to the Lord and eat and drink freely from His Word and Spirit, where the bread and living water run freely with no cost to your soul (John 7:37). Plus, constant Bible-reading reminds you that **you don't need to ask fear for permission to do what God has already purposed.**

# CHALLENGE:

Start today by reading all of Isaiah 55 in one sitting – yummy! Verse 11 is my favorite.*

# STOP ASKING FEAR FOR PERMISSION

to do what God has already purposed.

## Pinpoint Purpose:

Look at the church you attend. Write down which core values attracted you to it and why? (i.e. they value hospitality, they encourage or they creativity, or communicate Biblical messages clearly)

___

___

___

___

___

___

___

___

## DAY 6

**But he said to me, "My grace is sufficient for you, for my power is made perfect in weakness."**

*- 2 Corinthians 12:9*

It's so easy to leave church on Sunday rejoicing in God's goodness and then show up to work on Monday complaining about what we are lacking. Lord, we repent for our double-mindedness.

Is God really enough, or not? If He is, you must learn to filter the words you speak in unfavorable situations. God watches over His word to perform it – but if you are not declaring His words then it's hard for Him to move on your faithlessness. As pointed out in Hebrews 11:6, "without faith it is impossible to please God".

When your failures seem to be louder than God's promises, remember that your purpose was given to showcase His glory, not yours. So if you're feeling small for the task – you're the perfect candidate to receive His grace and strength.

## God gave you limitations so you'd focus on carrying out your purpose in partnership with Him, not solo.

That's also why He created prayer and granted you access to come before His throne boldly. This is a privilege that even angels do not have without meeting certain protocols. Don't waste it by turning to worry instead.

# CHALLENGE:

Bring to God any specific needs or areas of lack that have been discouraging you from progressing lately. He can handle it, there's enough grace for that.*

# YOUR PURPOSE FLOWS FROM YOUR FAITH

not your flaws.

## Pinpoint Purpose:

What do you quickly offer to do or help with for free? Write down 1-2 ways you can monetize these passions to free up yourself to produce more work in these areas.

_____
_____
_____
_____
_____
_____
_____
_____
_____

# DAY 7

"He humbled himself by becoming obedient."

– *Philippians 2:8*

There are no favorites in the kingdom of God except the humble. God gives grace to the humble, but the humbling part he leaves up to us. How do we do that? Believe and obey what He has said you can accomplish.

"Though you are little in your own eyes, are you not the head of Israel? The Lord anointed YOU king over Israel" (1 Samuel 15:17). This message from God to King Saul after his disobedience always encourages me. It reminds us that we are a big deal when God considers us worthy to assign us a task. Therefore, let's not reduce ourselves back down to people pleasing to feel important.

Be humble enough to be great at what God asked you to do.

Abandon any false humility or pretense. You are an ambassador of the Most High God. Yes, without Him we are nothing, but with Christ we are mighty in His grace and strength.

You were made new, so you can boldly be about your King's royal business.

## So when told you're acting brand new, smile and say "Thank you, I am."

# CHALLENGE:

Read Galatians 1:10 then ask the Holy Spirit to bring to mind any tasks you've procrastinated on because of what people may say. Ask His forgiveness and strength to do it this week with boldness. You're on God's side, why fear any man?*

# BE HUMBLE ENOUGH TO BE GREAT

at what God asked you to do.

## Pinpoint Purpose:

If you received a billion dollars, what's the first thing you would do to help others? Write down ways you can start serving in this area using what you can, where you are. Even if you don't have a billion dollars, God has given you something that someone else needs.

_____

_____

_____

_____

_____

_____

_____

_____

_____

# DAY 8

" It is for freedom Christ has set us free, stand firm therefore, and do not submit again to a yoke of slavery."."

*–Galatians 5:1*

Lionheart, before we can dive into your passions, this truth in this verse has to become your reality. It is for freedom you've been unchained from your sin – not for boredom, fear, or confusion. So why continue to live in those cages?

You were saved on purpose, for a purpose.
Believe the good report of the Lord and advance into the gifts, talents, and peace He has promised will "make room" for you (Proverbs 18:16).

Stop longing for Egypt and its fleeting delicacies. No matter how "good" the memories from your old life now seem, remember that you were a slave with no hope of knowing God intimately.

## God is greater than the sin He rescued you from

And He called you out by name so you could taste and see for yourself! Even more, He wants to give you good gifts so you can be an oasis in the earth. That way, others can pass through your life and experience His abundant kindness.

Boredom, fear, and confusion no longer have authority to bind you with their opinions, so feel free to look them in the eye today and say #ByeFelicia!

# CHALLENGE:

Take a picture of Galatians 5:1 on your phone and set it as your screensaver. Meditate on it throughout the day and try to say it from memory. Then declare it out loud whenever fear or confusion tell you that you have no purpose. Purpose begins with this essential ingredient - freedom!

**GOD** IS GREATER THAN **THE SIN** HE RESCUED YOU FROM.

## Pinpoint Purpose:

What passages in the Bible really get you excited or filled with hope? Look them up in your Bible or on Google, and write down 3-5 of the ones that really get you fired up.

_____

_____

_____

_____

_____

_____

_____

_____

## DAY 9

Jesus said to them, "My food is to do the will of him who sent me and to accomplish his work."

—John 4:34

What did God have in mind when He created you?

Without knowing this, everything you do will be a shot in the dark and a mere hoping for happily ever after. But when you realize that you have been specifically wired for success in a specific gifting and path living, becomes an easy yolk.

Your unique identity becomes a treasure that you guard with your life instead of pawning it for another "popular" option. And the spirit of the Lord becomes the very necessary fuel for solving that problem that you were sent here to resolve.

# Forget about missing out on the world - you're missing out on the real you

Jesus took the time to pinpoint His purpose before He jumped into ministry and fame, so it kept Him from getting weary or sidetracked when circumstances got hectic. In the same way, you must slow down and ask God to give you the direction and purpose for each season you find yourself. Find out who you are and why all your parts add up to a whole in God's eyes - because He makes all things well. There's nothing like knowing God's heart for you and those around you. Only then do you get excited about seeing it come to pass with each step of obedience. It brings a satisfaction like no other!

# CHALLENGE:

Imagine you just got sentenced to prison for the next 50 years. What are 3 things you're sad about not experiencing or completing? Now write them down and make your freedom count!

# YOU'RE MISSING OUT ON THE REAL YOU!

## Pinpoint Purpose:

What do friends and families always ask you to do for them? Write down whatever comes to mind. (i.e. plan events or fix laptop)

_____

_____

_____

_____

_____

_____

_____

_____

_____

## DAY 10

"You did not choose me, but I chose you and appointed you that you should go and bear fruit..."

−John 15:16

# Fitting in is not an option. You were chosen for this

As a daughter of the King, you have been called out for purpose. The Holy Spirit has now been given to you, so that you can stand out. Why smother such a royal mark to become relevant, when that's the best part about your new identity?

The Holy Spirit allows you to bring results to your culture and circle, which will in turn make you relevant to their needs. Not the other way around. Yet, we get so deceived into pursuing society's way of living, hoping we can then draw their attention to how relatable and good God is. But that's so unnecessary.

God is relatable and good, all by Himself.

Remember where your true influence and success comes from - from the Lord. And believe it or not, the world is actually watching to see if we as Christians will bring something different to the table to tackle today's many current issues. So it is foolish to cheat them, and yourself, by trying to hide the very thing that they need to see at work – the power of God at work in you.

Never apologize for pursuing what God has purposed you to do.

Even if you are not fully clear on what your specific gifts are, Isaiah 61:1 lets you in on your main purpose, no matter what season we're in. Your generation is desperately seeking supernatural answers and unshakeable love. It's time to plug into the Holy Spirit and shine!

# CHALLENGE:

Read Isaiah 61:1 then thank God for the gift of the Holy Spirit. Ask Him to fill you even more, so that you can carry out your main purpose to preach the good news and declare freedom to those around you.

# FITTING IN IS NOT AN OPTION

You were chosen for this.

## Pinpoint Purpose:

Write down a list of mentors or role models that you follow or pay attention to. How have they helped you grow or what about them do you admire?

_____

_____

_____

_____

_____

_____

_____

_____

_____

_____

## DAY 11

"Where there is no prophetic vision the people cast off restraint."

–Proverbs 29:18

Contrary to popular belief sis, seeing is not believing when you're in relationship with God. Instead, what you believe is what you will eventually see.

So if you can see it coming up in your mind frequently, you need to write it down. Then, as this vision becomes clearer, you'll find yourself restraining from distracting activities to pursue what you now believe is possible.

Having that vision written down starts helping you prioritize those passions in your schedule. And you'll begin searching for ways to sharpen your gifts so you can move closer to seeing the vision realized.

These purpose driven habits also give healthy direction to your desires, instead of letting them seep out in idle hands. For example, don't focus on not watching that TV show or not wasting hours on Instagram. Your mind will just keep spinning in guilt and defeat. Plus, those habits only return if the real issue of discontentment is not dealt with. Switch to the offensive instead and seek out God's joy and vision for your tasks each day (Psalm 145:16).

In other words, there really is no in between.

## Be purpose driven, or be wasting time

# CHALLENGE:

Create a vision board of words or images driving you towards your purpose. If you already have one, how can you refresh it to keep you motivated and excited towards your goals? Keeping your focus in front of you is important to avoid distractions and time-wasting.

# BE PURPOSE DRIVEN, OR BE WASTING TIME.

## Pinpoint Purpose:

What do you "waste time" doing when not on the job? Write down the projects or places that you escape to on your down time.

_____

_____

_____

_____

_____

_____

_____

_____

_____

## DAY 12

"..but where sin increased, grace increased all the more"

–Romans 5:20

With all the brokenness and perversion in the Earth, there is so much opportunity for the Holy Spirit to work. Not only is He able to move, but He is willing and waiting to act. However, will we walk in our identities as ambassadors in the earth and create space and elbow room for Him to work?

See, the heavens belong to the Lord, but the Earth He has given to the children of man (Psalm 115:16). So for earthly matters, God positions us as salt of the earth, to be channels of His grace. Let's not fear the increase of sin around us – it's why we're still here, so more light can shine in the darkness!

Practice praying with confidence for Him to use your words and actions to showcase His power over sin – not just in your life, but for all those in your sphere of influence. That's your awesome privilege and purpose.

# God's way works, so stop asking fear for permission to pursue your purpose

Trust Him and just start with the last thing He asked you to do.

# CHALLENGE:

Write down a sin struggle or fear that has been keeping you from using your gifts confidently. Decide to no longer let that guilt or shame keep you from God's ability to take you higher. Now pray and thank God for His promise that His grace will rise to match and overpower that resistance!

# GOD'S WAY WORKS,
so stop asking fear for permission to pursue your purpose.

## Pinpoint Purpose:

Which overlooked needs in your culture currently frustrate you? Write what you see as possible solutions or things not being done about it.

_____

_____

_____

_____

_____

_____

_____

_____

_____

# PINPOINT PURPOSE:

Review your answers to all twelve prompts to identify the 1-3 common themes. Now ask God to help you prioritize these passions with everything you do this season.

1. What issues in the overall church or Christian culture make you sad?
2. Is there a common struggle or need you tend to notice among your friends?
3. What advice do people always ask you for?
4. What do you see or imagine when you pray or daydream?
5. If you received a billion dollars, what's the first thing you would do to help others?
6. What do you quickly offer to do or help with for free?

7. Look at the church you attend – what core value attracted you to it? (i.e. they value hospitality, encourage creativity, or communicate Biblical messages clearly)
8. What passages in the Bible really get you excited or filled with hope?
9. What do friends and families always ask you to do for them? (i.e. plan events or fix laptop)
10. What type of mentors or role models do you admire?
11. What do you "waste time" doing... or escape to do on your down time?
12. Which overlooked needs in your culture currently frustrate you?

## UNCAGED
WITH ROBYN-ANN.COM

And remember, friends don't let friends live outside of purpose.
**Share the free challenge**
with someone who can benefit:
### ididitonpurpose.com